Y0-BRR-650

Packin' Up & Moving to Canada- 101

AN EXPERIENTIAL GUIDE FROM PRE-APPLICATION TO SETTLING IN AS A NEWCOMER TO CANADA

Nathalee D. Ferguson

PACKIN' UP & MOVING TO CANADA-101. Copyright © 2020. Nathalee D. Ferguson. All Rights Reserved.

Printed in the United States of America.

No portion of this book may be reproduced, stored in a retrieval system, or transmitted in any form or by any means, except for brief quotations in printed reviews, without the prior written permission of Nathalee D. Ferguson.

Cover Photograph:
Don Valley Parkway, Toronto (Ontario).

Photograph was captured and made available by photographer: ArJay.

Follow him on Instagram @mr._tade

ISBN: 978-1-949343-64-9 (paperback)

Packin' Up & Moving to Canada- 101

AN EXPERIENTIAL GUIDE FROM PRE-APPLICATION TO SETTLING IN AS A NEWCOMER TO CANADA

Nathalee D. Ferguson

Dedication

This book is dedicated to my mother Edna M. Ricketts. You have been a tower of strength and encouragement during the process of me migrating to and settling into my new life in Canada. When this dream to write a book was laid on my heart, you were very constant in reminding me that I always had a passion for writing and that authoring my own book was something I used to dream of doing as a child. Sometimes we humans run and hide from our dreams and at other times we get so caught up with societal notions of what constitutes a worthwhile career that we neglect other innate gifts. Your encouragement helped me stay the course when I had feelings of doubt along the way. Mother, you've reminded me, without even trying, that while we can run and hide from a calling, running is the mark of cowards.

I vividly remember when I first shared with you that I was planning to move to Canada. You were very concerned for yourself and for me but you were still quick to support my decision. I hope that this brave attempt to bare it all and share my story in order to help others will be demonstrative of the awesome job you have done raising me. Because of you, I am brave enough to chase every dream and knock down every wall in life. I thank you for your sacrifices and most of all for your unwavering love, laughter and belief in me.

Love and Blessings!

Contents

The Epiphany

Epiphany*- an illuminating discovery or an intuitive grasp of reality through something simple and striking* (Merriam Webster Dictionary)

Let me start this book with the 'why'. It's important to know your reason for moving before deciding to pack up and move to a foreign country. This was my 'why'.

2017 was an amazing year for me. I was approaching a milestone age, which caused me to be both nervous and excited about what the real 'big woman' stage of my life was going to look and feel like. My work, managing the missing children portfolio within the Government of Jamaica, was really benefiting from the kind of attention and action (to a large extent) that it deserved, and I was absolutely certain that I was in my dream job. Not only was I serving vulnerable children and their families, but I had just represented my country at two conferences for missing and exploited children, one in Winnipeg (Canada) and the other in Buenos Aires (Argentina). I was also already a Fulbright Alumni, having participated in the US State Department's International Visitor Leadership Program (IVLP) for emerging world leaders the year before. I found myself traveling a lot in my personal time and I was enjoying the company of great friends and family. I was living my best life…. or so I thought.

One afternoon early in June of that year, I sat by the window in my office at work and started questioning the direction of my life, and if I was truly living my "*best*" life or if I was just settling. I sat there that day and suddenly felt lacking, like there was so much more that I could achieve and, in that moment, I started to ask myself if I had gotten too complacent and if I was actually the culprit holding myself back from my true best self. Does that make sense? Can you relate? The truth is, although I was in a management job and while I was able to save a bit, I couldn't afford (as a single young professional) to buy my own home in Jamaica or even worse, if I were to have children at the time, I would not be able to maintain an acceptable lifestyle or give them the type of childhood I'd want for them.

This is so often the cry of many young and qualified persons in developing countries and so, in an effort to make the best of available opportunities to improve their lives, they migrate. In that same vein, it is equally worth noting how limited the market was in my home country for single, ambitious, well intentioned men who desired to love on a strong ambitious woman like myself. I felt that perhaps I needed a change of scenery so that the right man could find me. The Bible does say that 'he who finds a wife finds a good thing' right? I digress. Anyway, at that very moment, I had an epiphany, one of those 'aha' moments and started brainstorming my next adventure. I decided it was time to run out into the unknown and chase the best version of me, whatever that was supposed to be, look or feel like. I decided to step outside of my comfort zone for once and blaze a trail my unborn children will be absolutely proud of. I decided to pack up my life and migrate to Canada.

I was getting so excited about the limitless possibilities and found myself scouring the internet, researching everything about the express entry program and started making my plans. My mother was absolutely terrified when I told her about my intentions, and understandably so. She reminded me of how much I dread cold climates, and the fact we had just a handful of relatives in Canada, the majority of which I had never even met before. I started doubting myself for a while too. What if I failed at my attempt to get permanent residence (PR) after spending what I believed was going to be so much money? (At that time, I didn't know how much it would cost but figured it was a pretty penny). What if I gave up my normal and ran off to a foreign country (which I'd only ever been to once in my life) only to have regrets? If my last trip to Canada was anything to go by, why Canada???

Backstory: I arrived at the Sangster International Airport in Montego Bay, Jamaica on May 15, 2017 heading to the Winnipeg conference I mentioned earlier. I had traveled from Kingston the night before and I was completely drained after what felt like the longest, most horrid week of my life (I'm exaggerating). My flight (Air Canada 1805) was scheduled to land in Toronto for a connecting flight to Winnipeg later that night. While in the waiting area prior to boarding, I noticed a guy who appeared 'highly intoxicated'. It drew my attention because I had previously witnessed a similar situation while traveling across the US and that passenger was not allowed on the flight. So, I was a bit concerned when I saw him boarding the plane with the rest of us, but I was so tired that I actually fell asleep as soon as the plane took off. Perhaps an hour or so into the flight, I heard sounds which woke me from my very peaceful sleep. There was the same passenger, whose face I will never forget, in somewhat of a tussle with the flight attendants and a few male passengers who were trying to help restrain him. He seemed intent to 'bring down the plane' .... bring down which plane??? By this time, I was completely awake and alert... with my phone out and recording the melee hoping I would live to tell the tale. This was definitely not how I planned to exit the world.

Long story short, the flight had to be diverted to Orlando and the FBI escorted the then restrained passenger off the plane. I followed up on the case (since my life could have been lost in that mess) and read that he later pleaded guilty to having taken drugs, disrupting the flight and risking all our lives. Before all of that though, this situation resulted in a number of passengers including myself missing our connecting flights. I ended up getting to my hotel a day late and missing out on key presentations. Fortunately, when I arrived at my hotel, a movie was being filmed on site and guess who was starring in it? Keanu Reeves!! Mi glad bag buss! (translation: my excitement was uncontainable). I managed to sneak a few pictures of him and some with him in the background. Anyway…. I digress (again).

Some additional questions ran across my mind as I considered moving to Canada though. In retrospect though, those were the least of the many worries I have had to contend with since embarking on this journey. I was also concerned about the exorbitant fees that immigration consultants were charging interested persons. Some persons may be able to afford these fees and some were willing to even take loans for this but others, like myself, preferred to take the time and go through the steps myself. If the fees were more reasonable, I would perhaps have taken on the help to avoid me scrambling through the whole process but that was not the case. I went through the process without professional assistance and it took just a few months after I started the process to get confirmation of permanent residence. No doubt, you can do it too.

This short book is the product of sweat, sacrifice and 'nuff' (a lot of) tears. It is intended to serve as a simple conversational guide with all the relevant steps in migrating to Canada as a skilled professional. While this book will walk you through the steps involved and shed light on knowledge and insight I've gained through extensive secondary research and my own personal experience, it is critical that the reader understands his /her responsibility to do additional research to keep abreast of all the current changes that may take place from time to time. I have intentionally avoided going through some areas simply because I wanted to share what seems to cause most of the confusion and tips that you wouldn't quite find elsewhere. This book promises moments of outbursts in Jamaican patois as you have observed so far, but the appropriate translations will follow. I'm excited to share my Instagram account: "Moving2Canada101" and YouTube channel: "Packin' Up & Moving to Canada 101" where I will be posting photos and videos about life in Canada and respond to additional questions you may have. If you read anything and want me to further elaborate or if you want me to talk about other legitimate paths to migrating to Canada, feel free to keep in touch so I can share the deets (details)!

Finally, here is a quick run-down of the general areas we will be going through in the body of this book:

(I) Transcripts
(II) The Educational Credential Assessment
(III) Language Testing
(IV) The National Occupational Classification (NOC) system

(V) Options: The Express Entry Pool vs College
(VI) The Provincial Nominee Program
(VII) The invitation to apply for permanent residence
(VIII) Preparing to make the move
(IX) Settling in Canada

I am usually very private about my personal life, the paths I take as well as my mistakes and things of that nature (probably because of fear that some persons will tune in just to find something to laugh and gossip about). However, this book represents a transparency moment for me. I open up to share my own personal experiences with you so that you wont make the same mistakes I made along the way or be confused about the simple things that confused and delayed me. I know all too well that a lot of persons don't like to share the tricks and secrets and so they may share the very basic details that are common knowledge but they don't share the tips and insights gained that will make your experience easier than theirs. I want your experience throughout this process to be well informed and simple. Thanks for making me a part of your journey and, albeit inadvertently, supporting a dream I have had for years and a journey I have been trying to make sense of myself. I am nowhere near where I want to be on this Canadian journey of mine but so far this has definitely been a path worth walking.

With all of that said, cozy up in your favourite spot, grab a cup of Canada's favourite beverage (some good ole' coffee) and get ready to start your journey to Canada!

Getting Your House Together

Express Entry, Canada's flagship route to migration to Canada, has, in recent years, become perhaps the most popular method of migrating to Canada and for sure the quickest. The application process itself can be as short as three (3) months and my own application took exactly four (4) months to be processed. How do you know which program to apply through though? That part confused me initially and it has been a question I have been asked by everyone I have assisted with the express entry process so far.

There are three (3) programs: The Federal Skilled Worker Program, Federal Skilled Trades Program and the Canadian Experience Class. Although I will be focusing on the Federal Skilled Worker program in this book, it is important that I break down all three (3) so you are certain of where you fit.

The Federal Skilled Worker Program is a broad program geared at persons with post-secondary education and relevant work experience to help meet Canada's labour market needs. Applicants are assessed based on factors such as one's age, language skills, level of education and how easily it is expected that he/she can adjust or adapt to life in Canada. The Canadian Experience Class is, as the name suggests, for persons with Canadian work experience (of at least a year) within the last three (3) years before applying. The experience must first of all be legal (i.e under the table /cash jobs do not count) and must also be relevant to labour market needs. When discussing labour needs, we are speaking specifically of the Canadian National Occupational Classification (NOC) which is critical to an applicant being considered for permanent residence. I'll speak on this in more detail later in this chapter. The Federal Skilled Trades program in basic terms is for persons with actual skill trades eg. Electricians, Construction Tradesmen and Chefs to name a few. These individuals are required to have at minimum two (2) years full-time experience in an actual trade within the five (5) years preceding application.

Now, this may sound extremely cliche but the secret ingredient to this PR process is the preparation, and I'll stress that throughout this book. For me, it took months to get everything together before I moved ahead with actually expressing my interest to Immigration, Refugee and Citizenship Canada (IRCC). I learned, particularly in getting my credentials assessed, that rushing was a complete mistake. Maybe I am just not great at dealing with information overload, but I found out that speed gets you nowhere far with this process. Take your time and… get your house together.

Language Testing

The first thing I did in this entire process was to sign up for an exam date for language testing. Generally, language test dates are hard to come by because of the high demand for available spots and the limited capacity of any given test center to accommodate a large number of candidates in one sitting. I booked my language exam at the start of June when I had my 'aha' moment and the earliest available date in my country (Jamaica) was November of that year. With this in mind, look online for the earliest date possible and do not delay too much.

For the Federal Skilled Worker Program, the minimum average of the four (4) test areas: speaking, writing, reading and listening is the Canadian Language Benchmark (CLB) of 7. This translates to a score of six (6) across all four (4) components of the IELTS language test or a score of seven (7) across all four (4) components of the CELPIP language test. For the Federal Skilled Trades Program, the minimum score is CLB 4 for reading and writing and CLB 5 for speaking and listening. For the IELTS language test, the minimum scores that one would have to attain therefore is 3.5 for reading, 4.0 for writing, and 5.0 for listening and speaking. For the CELPIP language test, it would mean a minimum score of 4 for reading and writing and 5 for speaking and listening. Your CRS points for the language component of your overall score is critical so you have to prepare prepare prepare.

Here are some tips I learned along the way regarding the language test:

Tip #1: If you are willing and able to, you can look into doing the language test in another country. For example, my younger cousin was able to secure a date in Miami (USA) in a much shorter time while a friend of mine did her language test in New York (USA) while visiting her mother for Christmas. Many persons seem to be of the view that they are confined to doing language testing in their country but, although travelling to another country will cost money, it is an option available if you have a tight timeline working with.

Tip #2: You do NOT have to do the IELTS language test. Yes, it is perhaps the more popular English option but the CELPIP is just as simple and it is an IRCC approved language test. In fact, the test is administered by a group which I read is a subsidiary of the University of British Columbia in Canada, so it is definitely 'legit'. Some persons prefer paper testing and so the electronic nature of the CELPIP may not be ideal, but the truth is that it does not matter which of the two you do (i.e. IELTS or CELPIP). I did the IELTS and got good scores but I also helped a friend go about doing the CELPIP when her IELTS scores had expired after two (2) years and she wasn't able to secure a realistic test date locally. In actuality, she ended up doing a bit better with the CELPIP than she did at the IELTS two (2) years prior. I asked her to compare the two (since she did both) and this is what she said verbatim:

*"Neither of the two is easier than the other in terms of difficulty because it is really the same test. One is written (IELTS) and one is computerized (CELPIP). The difficulty will depend on personal preferences and skills. For example, with the IELTS listening test, you listen to the recording and scribble things on paper while you listen. For the CELPIP, you listen to things in the very same way but, if I recall correctly, you would have to type what you need to scribble down"- **Nadia***

At the end of the day, what matters is the amount of preparation you put in. As Nadia said, both tests are more alike than they are different. If you have basic computer skills, you should be able to complete the CELPIP with ease. Deciding between the two (2) should be based on convenience (where you are physically located) and the time frame within which you are operating (i.e. when you need to have your test completed).

Tip #3: Persons whose first language is not English (or French) often feel intimidated because they are being tested in a language that is foreign to them, and the trepidation is understandable. I can assure you that there is no need to be anxious. Study materials are provided to you once you sign up for the exam and the trick is to focus more on what is being asked or what is required and not so much on being perfect. Example: I had a hard time in my speaking test even though I believe that I have somewhat of an advanced command of the English language. At the end of the exam, I asked the examiner what the examiners are really looking for. She said it wasn't a matter of me not speaking well but that I appeared more caught up with finding the best arguments and knowing facts as opposed to focusing on just the conversational aspect. I did well at that component of the IELTS, but I guess she realized I was giving way too many facts and overthinking the whole thing. The examiners want to know that you can communicate in English, not necessarily defend a PhD dissertation to them. If you can barely speak English, my advice is to book language classes as soon as (or before) you book the exam date and spend the waiting period improving on your English language skills so you are better prepared and more confident going into the exam.

Tip #4: The language test is not just for non-English speakers to worry about. The best piece of advice I got and can give to a native English speaker is to practice practice practice. Far too often I see persons do their language exam and take for granted that because they already speak English, the exam will be a walk in the park. I studied for the exam in advance and then almost all night the night prior to the exam to ensure I was able to give it my all and I was not able to get the scores I expected I'd have gotten. It was a hugely humbling experience for me and a useful reminder that even native English speakers are not perfect. Practice under test conditions and learn what the examiner would expect to be the 'most correct' response. That is something I struggled with during my studying. What made one answer more correct than mine? Because I added or removed one adjective? I realized that when you practice from the study materials and analyze the suggested answers, it gets easier to predict what they expect to be the most correct answer.

If you are going the Express Entry route to Canada, you must sit the 'General Training' option of the IELTS or the CELPIP General test. Individuals who specifically want to pursue academics before applying for permanent residence have to select the Academic option of the IELTS. In my research, I did not see where there is an academic version of the CELPIP. Since the foci of this book is on the express entry route to Canada, I will rarely mention the academic route as I find it easier and cheaper for persons with post-secondary qualifications and work experience to go the express entry route. Interestingly, I had gotten through for college in Canada back in 2013 when I already had my bachelors and masters degrees but I opted out of it for the same reasons I advise against it now for professionals who already qualify for Express Entry:

1. Not only do you still have to show proof of funds, but in the long run it may cost you much more because of interest rates on student loans when you consider the actual cost for international students.

2. College will be far more expensive for you as an international student and can cost anywhere in the ballpark of $30,000 CAD annually whereas citizens and permanent residents pay a small fraction of that. In addition to your tuition, you would also need to have $10,000 CAD as proof of funds. For an additional family member, a further $4,000 CAD is required as proof. This option adds up!

3. Permanent residence would take you significantly longer to get because following the conclusion of your studies, you would then have to apply for a post-graduation work permit (cost: $255 CAD) which will, if granted, be valid for a period dependent on the number of years you studied at an approved learning institution. At no point during your studies or with a

work permit do you qualify for government health insurance and, healthcare is very costly in Canada.

4. While studying, there are restrictions on the number or hours you can work. You are limited to working for twenty (20) hours per week. This part is very serious. In December 2017, a very promising foreign student was arrested because he was found to have worked for more than twenty (20) hours. I stumbled upon the article in June 2019 and was heartbroken about the circumstances and his fate as it had been announced in May 2019 that a decision was made and he was going to be deported. This was a student with no known prior convictions and was said to have been an excellent student. Yes, many persons may be lucky enough to get away with working for longer periods than allowed but I would not recommend you take such a risk as this could affect your chances of permanent residence in the country in the long run.

Education Credential Assessment

The second thing I did was to pay for my Education Credential Assessment (ECA) report and this was where I got a bit too hasty. I was so overwhelmed to the point that I did not do enough research to understand the differences between the approved designated organizations because I felt I was in a race to get my documents together.

IRCC requests that applicants submit an ECA report if the applicant received his/her education outside of Canada. This is to help them determine if your degree is equivalent to one issued in Canada. While you do not need to get all your degrees assessed (just the highest one), you get a score for multiple degrees so if for instance you have a masters degree or doctoral degree, you will get additional points for them if they are deemed equivalent to these degrees in Canada. Woot Woot!! For fields outside of the medical arena, these are the approved bodies:

1. International Credential Assessment Service of Canada (ICAS)

2. World Education Services (WES)

3. International Qualifications Assessment Service (IQAS)

4. Comparative Education Service (CES) (U of T School of Continuing Studies)

5. International Credential Evaluation Service (ICES)

Honestly, I selected ICAS based on the aesthetics of their website. It looked a bit more professional than WES did in my estimation at the time and so I ran with them. What I liked about WES though (after actually doing my due diligence) was the fact that their processing times were much shorter and that they frequently shared resources and hosted free webinars for persons who have an interest in working or studying in Canada.

After paying the non-refundable fee to ICAS, I discovered that their processing time was a whopping five (5) months. I was livid but, because my language test was already set for November, I soon got over it. I ended up learning too that literally everyone who I knew had used WES and that their reports were available in mere weeks.

Due to my haste, I had to wait for five (5) months hoping my masters and bachelors degrees were going to be deemed equivalent to those degrees in Canada. Thankfully, I got a professionally prepared report within their estimated timeframe saying just that.

So, what are the fees and processing times for each of the organizations after they accept documents and deem them 'complete'?

ICAS- Timeline: 25 weeks. Fees: $200 CAD plus courier fees. I submitted both degrees for assessment and the price remained at $200 CAD.

WES- Timeline: 35 business days. Fees: $220 CAD plus HST (harmonized sales tax) and courier fees ranging from $7 to $85 CAD)

IQAS- Timeline: About 20 weeks. Fees: $200 CAD (regardless of number of credentials) plus courier fees ($15 CAD inside Canada, $75 CAD outside of Canada). IQAS is based in Alberta and I have seen employers who required an IQAS education credential assessment report as part of their application process.

CES- Timeline: 12 weeks. Fees: $210 CAD plus courier fees)
ICES- Timeline: Usually 20 weeks but based on their website, due to a high applicant volume from Africa, this may take longer. Fees: $200 per credential with courier fees ($26 CAD within Canada and $75 CAD outside of Canada)

NOC Codes

Another critical preparatory step that I would have hinted at earlier is to determine your "NOC code". A part of you proving that you would be an economic asset to the country is your ability to link your skill sets with fields that are 'in demand' in Canada. Well, what is a 'NOC' code? 'NOC' stands for National Occupational Classification. This system classifies different job functions and places them under broad categories which are used by Statistics Canada and IRCC to speak on labour market needs. The beauty of the NOC codes is that it is rare that you only fit within one (1) code. In fact, I found that I had fit under a few based on my skills/ education and experience. You simply have to have at least one (1) year of full time experience working in a role that matches with that NOC code for the last ten (10) years and you are 'good to go'.

I decided on the code I wanted to use based on labour needs and used that when I was entering the express entry pool.

Based on my assessment of IRCC immigration reports for 2017 and 2018, the most popular fields invited for permanent residence were Information Technology related (including computer programmers and software engineers) followed by food services. This is not to say that other fields were not in demand, but these were the 'most popular' statistically.

Jumping in the Pool... Can you Swim?

After all the preparatory work at this point, you are ready to jump on into the pool of candidates vying for a coveted invitation to apply for permanent residence. According to the official site of the Canadian government, candidates are ranked using a points-based system called the Comprehensive Ranking System (CRS).

My comprehensive ranking score (CRS) was 473 broken down as follows:

CRS- Human Capital- Age 105 points (30 years old)

CRS- Human Capital- Education 135 points (M.Sc highest level of education)

CRS- Skills Transferability- Education- 50

CRS- Skills Transferability- Foreign Work Experience- 50

Now, had I applied prior to turning 30, I would have been able to get five (5) points more than I got for the age component of the CRS. Had my sibling been a resident of Canada and not the United States of America, I would have gotten an additional fifteen (15) points. Had I been proficient in French as well, thirty (30) additional points for that and better yet, had I gotten a job offer in Canada, I would have gotten between fifty (50) and two hundred (200) extra points. Having Canadian education helps you score higher as well.

Personally, I did not want to get a provincial nomination but for persons with lower scores, this is certainly an additional option to consider.

Flexibility is therefore something that persons need, particularly when their score is not as competitive in the pool. The issue though is that a provincial nomination means you must commit to living in the province which invited you for a minimum of two (2) years. Do NOT accept a provincial nomination unless you are willing to commit to living in the province that invited you. Do a google search on the provinces and see where your skillsets are needed and determine if that is an area where you are willing to live.

I remember googling provinces such as Nunavut, Manitoba, New Foundland and Labrador among others and I was not interested. This is by no means to bash these territories but, for me, I thrive when I am closer to friends and family as well as Caribbean cuisine and culture. Based on some of the other issues I faced after moving (including depression), my family and friends in Canada kept me sane during the first six (6) months. Just as critical in decision making was the fact that I preferred to settle in a province where it was not as cold as some other provinces. At a point in my application process, I thought I would move to Alberta and that is exactly what I had communicated to IRCC but then 'life happened' and I ended up in Ontario.

Now, I don't know anyone who received a provincial nomination so I wont profess to be an expert where nominations are concerned. Generally, persons are invited based on high demand fields and it is by no means the case that these unpopular provinces are just desperately calling for applicants. IRCC encourages persons to reach out to provinces they have an interest in so for those needing additional points, the Provincial Nominee Program (PNP) is a good bet. The downside (in my opinion) is that PNP invitations are said to take a longer time to be processed. These are definitely factors to consider while floating around in the pool.

Perhaps the best advice I can give while you wait is to assess the trends carefully and determine if you need to do anything to improve on your score. In fact, one of the best things you can possibly do is to start learning French if you are not already fluent in French. You might be thinking how unrealistic this is for what may be a short period of time, but not learning French ahead of time was my main regret. I have since missed out on so many job opportunities simply because I am not bilingual YET. Bilingualism in Canada is not just useful for you to get a higher score but it can also help you secure coveted jobs when you get to Canada since you would be able to communicate in both of Canada's official languages and serve a wider cross section of people. In the event your English language score requires improvement, that is also something you can consider in the interim if needed.... and only if needed. Don't become encumbered with doing unnecessary things but be open to improving your chances if you find your scores are lower than average. If you have a score of at least 440-450, there is usually nothing to worry about. It is highly likely that there will be a round in which you are invited to apply for permanent residence and therefore you do not need to get caught up with panic. As I often tell persons, don't get "boomy" (overly impatient).

A friend of mine and his wife applied together. Both of them possessed bachelors degrees and years of experience in their fields. I don't know their precise circumstances, but their collective score was 402. They waited in the pool for months and nothing happened. Fortunately, they possessed the financial means to try the more expensive route and he eventually came to Canada and pursued a graduate certificate. The college option is therefore a back-up alternative if you have excess money to spare.

Comparative Review of CRS Scores 2017-2019

The CRS score was a hot button topic for me while I waited to be invited under the Federal Skilled Worker program of Express Entry. After my big blunder and ultimate letter regarding being ineligible to apply under the federal skilled worker program in January 2018 (due to me being too hasty and putting the wrong NOC code), I was formally invited to apply for PR on March 14, 2018 as soon as I entered the pool that month. The cutoff score for that draw was 456 which was the highest cutoff score for the entire year. As I shared earlier, my score was 473 so when I read about the cutoff score, I knew I was invited and made my way over to my email for the notification message in my account.

While 456 was the highest cut off score used in all of 2018, the lowest score was 440. The average score (minus the two program specific draws for the year) was 443 over the twenty-five (25) regular draws held. In fact, the most frequently occurring scores were 440 and 442 (which were the cut off scores five times each during the year) followed by 441 which was the cut off score four times that year. The year started with the January 10 draw with a cutoff score of 446 and ended with the December 19 draw with a cutoff score of 439 which also happened to be the lowest cutoff score (aside from program specific draws) of the year. If we should compare these scores to 2017, we will notice what may appear to be a yearly increasing of the cut off scores. The lowest score of 2017 was 415 which was the cut off score for April 19 and May 17. That year (2017) started off with 468 as the first cut off score in the January 4 draw (which was also the highest for the year) and closed off with 446 in the December 20 draw. The average cutoff score (minus the four program specific draws) was 438 and there was just one more draw in 2017 than in 2018. What we must be cognizant of is the fact that with more applicants, many of whom are highly qualified, the threshold will naturally change to suit the dynamics of the individuals in the pool hence higher cut off scores year over year. As at Christmas Eve 2019, the lowest cutoff score was 438 and the highest was 475.

Chapter 4

So, you've been invited to apply for Permanent Residence... What next?

As soon as you receive your invitation to apply for permanent residence, you have sixty (60) days to submit all necessary documents through the IRCC account portal. If you miss this deadline, you will have to re-enter the pool and wait to be invited all over again. It is therefore critical that you try your very best to get started with gathering the required documents as soon as you receive your invitation to apply. The key documents you will need are:

Passport/Travel Document
Copy of Degree(s)
Employment letters
Medical Report
Police Certificate
ECA Report
Proof of Funds
Photograph

Your travel document, photograph and degree(s) might be the easiest on the list to source since you would have those documents on hand and could quite easily scan and save them to your laptop/ computer in advance. While you will need to insert details regarding your language test report, you will not have to attach the actual language report to your account. You will however have to upload your ECA report for review.

Employment Letter

In addition to the other documents you would have ahead of time, you could also request job letters from listed employers beforehand so that vacation or unplanned absences on the part of their human resource (HR) personnel will not affect your sixty (60) day timeline. The IRCC website states that pay stubs can be used to substantiate your history at a particular company. This is useful in cases where the company is no longer in operation or in similar situations that would result in you not being able to get documentation proving past employment. One of the companies I had listed had gone through so many mergers since my resignation that the HR department simply could not trace so far back to find a record of me working there. Equally terrifying for me was the fact that another company had archived all employee files older than five (5) years and indicated that they were unable to assist me in the required timeframe. Fortunately, I had copies of all my pay stubs as far back as 2008 and so I prepared a letter of explanation and attached the first and last pay stub as well as my signed offer of employment, job description and a copy of the email from the HR department detailing the situation. This was sufficient for IRCC.

In terms of format, the employment letter has to be on official letterhead and must include your job title, start and end date, salary, and main duties performed. To ensure that your letter helps support your application under the NOC code you selected, make sure that HR indicates the specific functions within your job description that you absolutely need in that letter so that the IRCC agent processing your application will be able to see that you have the relevant experience to be applying with that code. Remember that you were invited to apply based on that occupational code in the first place so the experience outlined in these letters must substantiate your claim.

Medical Examination

The medical examination will also need to be done for your application to be considered. On the www.canada.ca website, you will be able to find the closest panel physician(s) authorized to perform a medical examination in your country. Your family doctor will therefore not be able to do the examination for you unless he or she is on the list of authorized physicians. In addition to the doctor's physical assessment, you will do a chest X-ray and a blood test. At some point during this visit, the physician will give you a printout which you will upload to prove from your end that the medical examination was completed. The actual results will be sent from the physician directly to IRCC. Lately, I have heard of occasional delays with getting prompt appointments and I have a friend who recently had to wait for two weeks for an appointment. To be on the safe side, contact the physician's office within a day of being invited to apply for permanent residence. If there is a delay, you will be better able to manage it and, if you suffer from trypanophobia (fear of needles) like me, you can book a date that will be most ideal within the timeframe you are working with.

Police Certificate

Another really important step is to secure your police certificate. Just as you would have to do with the medical report, if you do not have the police certificate ready within the sixty (60) day window, you will have to decline your invitation. For the police certificate, if you have spent more than six (6) months in total in another country (irrespective of whether these months would have been consecutive or not), you will need police certificates for the country or countries you had been living. Summer vacations overseas do not count. This timeframe is applicable for periods of time after the age of eighteen (18). You will upload the police certificate in the appropriate section of your PR application.

Proof of Funds

The most critical of these steps for many is the proof of funds. I had absolutely no clue as to how I would have been able to put the required funds together and so I started brainstorming to see if I would be able to use a letter showing monies that were to be paid to me in the following months to a possible gift deed from my parents and if I can be completely honest, I intentionally delayed my application for months trying to find a way around the money situation. After a while, I realized that I did not need to have the required funds at the time of entering the pool. I spoke to a number of persons who went through the Express Entry program and I also did a lot of reading online to see what others had to do to meet this requirement. At the time of my application, I think the required funds was set at $12,000 CAD. I literally had it all together probably a week before I uploaded all my documents and submitted my complete application for permanent residence.

Proof of funds depends on the number of persons in your household (including your children) and usually increases annually. For 2019, the requirement was:

Number of Family Members	Funds Required (in Canadian dollars)
1 (Applicant Only)	$12,669
2	$15,772
3	$19,390
4	$26,701
5	$30,114

See full table at www.canada.ca

I heard of persons who took loans to show as proof of funds and got through with their application but honestly I advise against that. To be as frank as I possibly can, after starting over as a single person in Canada, I found that for you to settle in Canada, you will need far more than the funds required as proof of funds by IRCC. I recommend that you focus on getting your money together before even entering the pool but if not possible, continue doing any possible thing that is legal to get your funds together. IRCC does not care when you get the complete funds, just ensure that at the time of submitting the documents for your PR application, you have the funds in your account. By funds, we are not talking funds you expect in the future or funds in a fixed deposit account or stocks and bonds. IRCC requires ready cash… cash you can pull and go, literally!

The letter you need to get from your financial institution must be on official letterhead with the bank's contact information. It should also include your name, date your account was opened, average balance for the last six (6) months, current balance and all outstanding debts including credit card balances and loans. This is to ensure that you are not taking a loan to show as proof of funds.

I found myself in a very interesting predicament where the proof of funds issue was concerned. Looking at it now, this was not really a predicament but at the time I thought it was. I was expecting some money owed to me which would, when added to the savings I had at the time, exceed the amount required. The problem was the fact I also had a liability in the form of my car loan. In fact, my car loan was more than the required funds, so I thought I was operating at a deficit. Some persons told me that they did <u>not</u> disclose their car loans or mortgage to IRCC in order to avoid being denied on the basis of insufficient funds. I read in forums online that persons had included theirs and got through which gave me some hope about being completely honest in my application. A car loan for instance is, in simple terms, a temporary liability paid for by future income. You can quite easily sell your car to clear your loan and move on. I really am not certain if the same applies where a mortgage is concerned but I realized that IRCC is not as concerned about your debts as they are about ensuring you truly have the funds needed to settle in Canada.

Like many other persons, I used to think the actual process to apply for permanent residence in Canada was so expensive and that I would have to fork out what would translate to millions in my currency. With this view, I doubted ever being able to afford to migrate to Canada but somehow knew that if I was to end up here, I would, at the right time. At the end of the day, the overall cost itself (actual fees you have to pay IRCC) is minimal. For one (1) person, there is the Permanent Resident Application Fee $550 CAD and the Right of

Permanent residence fee $490 CAD as well as a small biometrics fee. Citizens from some countries (including Jamaica) are required to have their biometrics taken and the biometrics remain valid for ten (10) years. For the entire PR process, the police certificate, medical report, IELTS/CELPIP exam, ECA report, biometrics, PR Application fee and Right of PR fee are the things you will have to pay for. Yes, these all add up a bit, but you can just count it as an investment in yourself. Let this prepare you to face the expensive journey you are embarking on and the opportunities (I think) you are unlocking by deciding to move to Canada.

Now after submitting your application, relax! The wait time isn't fixed and so you could be waiting for as little as two (2) or three (3) months or as long as eight (8) months or more like a friend of mine who got her 'golden email' exactly eight (8) months after submitting her application. She sent emails to IRCC following up, even getting a reply once basically thanking her for keeping future emails at a minimum. This was so savagely hilarious that we laughed when she received it. She even paid for the GCMS notes (applicant status reports from IRCC) which I still don't believe was helpful since appropriate status updates are visible in the applicant's account.

According to the annual Express Entry year-end reports for 2016, 2017 and 2018, the average processing times for 80% of applications received for permanent residence were as follows:

Year	Federal Skilled Worker	Federal Skilled Trades	Canadian Experience Class
2016	6 months	6 months	6 months
2017	4 months	6 months	4 months
2018	6 months	7 months	5 months

It may take some time due to the volume of applicants but based on what I have seen, as long as you are qualified and experienced with a clean bill of health, your settlement funds and a clear travel and police record, you should be good to go. Fingers crossed!

Chapter 5

Packin' Up and Moving to Canada 101

Congrats on being offered Permanent Residence!! Here begins a new and exciting journey in a whole new country. This is where the mixed emotions will kick in. You literally will be packing up your life and moving to Canada!

Stated in your Confirmation of Permanent Residence (COPR) will be your deadline to land in Canada. Do not plan to land after that date as your document and temporary visa will, after that date, be expired and invalid. Usually, the deadline is around the time of the one (1) year anniversary of your medical report so you should plan to travel before that expires. This means that the length of time for processing usually impacts the landing date. For me, I got seven (7) months before my deadline to land in Canada after getting through with my PR application while Nadia barely got three (3) full months.

So, what do you pack? What will you absolutely need before you leave your home country? I'll share two (2) key things that will save you time and money. Firstly, you need to visit your local Ministry of Transportation and request a drivers abstract/ drivers history report. In Jamaica, I got this letter from the Island Traffic Authority. The letter essentially stated my name, address, the type of vehicles I am licensed to drive in Jamaica, license class along with drivers license number and dates of issue, renewal and expiration. In addition, the letter should state whether or not you have outstanding violations such as tickets as well as if your license has been suspended, revoked or has any endorsements that would be worth noting. I paid the necessary administrative fees, in my case at the tax office and then took my receipt and drivers license to Island Traffic Authority. I provided them with the address for the Drive Test Centre that was closest to where I would be staying in Canada and the letter itself took less than three (3) business days to be prepared, signed and stamped.

I left Jamaica with my Honda HRV parked in my mom's driveway. At the time I migrated, I wasn't certain that I would definitely stay in Canada, especially if things did not work out for me. I was split 50/50 to be honest and did not even resign from my government job in Jamaica but rather took a leave of absence. By the time I decided to settle in Canada on that first attempt and move forward with selling my car, I had the tough situation of having to find a solution for selling my car without actually having to physically sign over the ownership back in Jamaica. My solution was quite expensive, particularly because I had to do it from Canada and have it couriered to Jamaica. In order to have someone else handle your affairs as I had to do, you need to prepare a Power of Attorney prior to leaving your home country. Yes, you may have to pay to get one prepared for you by an

Attorney to ensure it meets the legal requirements of your country and the person to whom you have given this authority will then be able to be your 'hands and feet', for lack of a better term, while you are in Canada.

Before packin' up and leaving, you also need to (if you haven't gotten a job offer) do a great deal of research on possible cities to move to based on your field and the job market. What I currently pay monthly to rent a one bedroom apartment in the Greater Toronto Area (GTA) is almost double the amount paid by persons in less populated provinces. Funny enough, I had no intention of moving to Ontario and had in fact put Edmonton, Alberta on my PR application as I stated before. As fate would have it, I had no job at the time, nor did I have anywhere to stay in Edmonton. Consequently, I ended up in Ontario which has been the best thing for me given all that has happened since I migrated. Aside from that, I have had a rude awakening by the weather after actually living here and I've come to learn that the weather is even harsher outside of the GTA. If you are brave enough to pack up and start over your life though, why not take a leap of faith and try to find a job in Moncton, New Brunswick or Edmonton, Alberta or even in Ottawa, Ontario where I am told most government jobs are. Be open to somewhere you have no friends or connections if you are brave enough. I tend to get job alerts daily from Indeed.ca as well as other popular job sites and the highest paying jobs all seem to be in areas that are a bit further outside of Toronto and Vancouver (which, by the way, is BEAUTIFUL). Independence really pays off too. As I have been saying in the last few months "People want you to do well, until you start doing well." Not everyone wants to see you come to Canada and succeed especially in a timeframe that is shorter than theirs was so do not become anyone's burden. Find that opportunity and be open to different places where you can get a clean start.

Do you intend to transport anything by sea? Given that you will be migrating, there are customs related provisions to ensure that you are not unduly charged for transporting your important items. Should you opt to move with certain belongings including furniture, feel free to do so. In order for you to avoid customs fees, you must declare this during your interview after landing and you will receive the necessary documentation which you will take with you when collecting the items. To be honest though, that process may not make a lot of sense unless you already have really high end items that are worth shipping. Let's say you are going to stay with family initially or let's say you found a temporary job in a particular province to begin with, what will your plan be to move your belongings from Point A to Point B if you bring your whole 'house and land'? Transporting furniture across Canada can be quite costly. Do your research to see how much it would cost to transport what you want to take, decide if it is worth it and move forward with the facts. Whatever you do, do not plan to take your car with you, just in case that is even a thought. It can really be a hassle especially if it is a right-hand drive vehicle. Some insurance companies do not even insure vehicles that are right-hand drive.

Depending on the time of year you plan to migrate, arguably one of the most important things to do beforehand is to buy at least one (1) solid winter jacket and a sturdy pair of winter boots. Winters in Canada can get extremely brutal and for that reason, you need to get your winter gears together so you can physically survive it. I tried purchasing small things like scarves, gloves and tuques (a warm knitted cap with a tassel) while vacationing in the USA prior to migrating but limited my jacket and boot purchases to just a few light ones because I felt I needed jackets built specifically for the Canadian weather. I've been told that the best times to purchase winter gears at low prices would be at the end of the winter season which would be around end of March into April. For winter boots, I got a lot of feedback from Canadians either in department stores or at work. Sorel was the shoe brand I got most favorable reviews on. For winter jackets, I heard of Moose Knuckle, Canada Goose, Columbia, TNA and others.

The thing is, a Moose Knuckle jacket for instance usually starts at around $800 CAD for a standard jacket. The ideal winter jacket in that brand will be a few hundred dollars more than that but the brand is highly recommended so it must be really warm. I wouldn't advise you to break the bank for a jacket though although jackets are critical especially if you do not drive but I would say focus more on the description of the item because you may be able to find a brand that costs a bit less but offers the same superior protection as high end brands. My first winter jacket is from a vegan brand called Noize. I've heard great reviews about the brand and the jacket is advertised as capable of withstanding up to -30 degree C temperatures. One of the reviews I read online was from someone in Alberta who said the jacket can sometimes make her feel a little hot and so she only uses hers when it is one of the worst days. A Jamaican proverb I've always loved goes as follows:

"Fish go water Batam an seh it deep, believe him"
English translation: If a fish goes to the bottom of the water, comes back and says it is deep, believe him.

Alberta is known to have some of the most brutal winters and I've seen videos of snow storms even during summer in Alberta. With that said, I took the chance with the jacket. If an Albertan can say the jacket made her feel hot, I am almost certain this brand is worth making 'noize' about. See what I did there? I will share a possible review on the jacket closer to the end of my first winter ☺

Lastly, when does your passport or other important documents expire? Before heading off, get everything up to date because you will be away for at least a few months and you do not want to have to be scurrying to update these from abroad. Sure, most countries have consulates abroad where passport services can be handled but there are some things that must be done locally. Determine if this applies to you and make the necessary adjustments to your schedule to allow you to get things up to date prior to leaving. This is going to be an adventure with its fair share of processes and stress, so avoid the complications of having to add these kinds of tasks to your to-do list and just get it done before you pack up and go.

Jus Touch Down

Your Telephone Number

Announcement: Please be advised that you are not guaranteed permanent residence with your COPR document. Until you actually land in Canada, successfully complete your landing interview and have the landing details filled in on said document by the immigration officer, you are not a permanent resident. When I was waiting to be interviewed, I overheard the interviews for some other new immigrants in line and I recall seeing a couple and a student being asked to wait for some kind of further questioning. Canada ensures that they carefully determine who they give entry into to their country and what they allow you to take on their soil.

This realization led me to understand why I had such a hard time securing a job before I migrated. I found out that a part of the reason why some employers do not contact you while you are outside of the country is in fact because of several realities: the reality that they may waste time selecting you and then have lengthy delays having to wait on you to get to the country and to get settled or to start the recruitment process all over again if you do not get your 'landed' status. I have heard that in very rare cases, persons do not get through with their landing but that is usually in instances of material changes including adding a spouse afterwards, or issues with funds etc.

Almost as soon as I landed, I visited the mall with my friend 'Shines' and hop scotched between phone carriers to weigh my options. I had the option of getting a Toronto area code or a Barrie area code and I chose Barrie because of the flexibility to choose the last four (4) digits of my number if I did so. This was really convenient but proved to be a bit problematic after. I recently shared my business cards with some established professionals and one of the individuals immediately asked me if I live in Barrie. She was quick to encourage me to change my number ASAP to reflect that I actually do live in the GTA because employers consider location when shortlisting applicants. This was spot on advice. I recall a friend sharing with me why he did not even put his Mississauga address on his resume even though Mississauga is in the GTA. He applied for an entry level job with a particular delivery company in Vaughan and despite the fact both cities are just a highway away, he was told that was a deterrent to him being hired because of the known difficulties with commuting during periods of poor weather conditions. Since that experience, he never included his address in his applications.

The conversation I had about my own area code helped me understand some of the key issues that employers find with candidates who will undoubtedly have a tough commute to work. The truth is, the commute across the GTA can be hell, especially during winter which makes the applicant instantly seem potentially unreliable and appear as someone who will be leaving the job as soon as they get something closer to home. We all know that many of us have, at some point, submitted mass applications out of desperation. I have applied for jobs in the past and, looking back at it now, I'm not sure how I would have managed with commute. When I started my first job in Canada, I was commuting from North York to Mississauga by public transportation and it took me two buses and a train ride to get to work in two and a half (2.5) hours one way. That was a whopping five (5) hours plus my eight (8) hour work day to add to that.

Area codes apparently stand out also because of long distance charges. My friend could be outside my apartment building calling me from her cell phone and because I have a Barrie area code, she is billed for a long distance call. Another friend downloaded a particular application that provided her with a Toronto area code so that is something you can consider while you are outside of Canada i.e. getting a number with the area code of the city you will be moving to. The chances of you getting an invitation to an interview prior to landing is unlikely BUT not impossible. I actually got called for a very attractive position in Edmonton prior to moving but that fell through because I had listed my friend's mobile number and she retrieved the voice message too late. I'd recommend that you download one of those apps to start your job hunt and ensure you choose an area code specifically for the territory you want to work.

The First Week

There is no real deadline to get your health card, driver's license etc but I recommend that you get these done as soon as you land because when you start working, which could be within a month or worst case scenario up to a year, you may not be able to get the time off to do these things. The first thing I'd suggest you do is to head to Service Canada to get your social insurance number (also called S.I.N but I never refer to it as such!). It will be quite a wait (especially in highly populated cities) so bring snacks with you and a good book or just ensure your phone is fully charged. On average, it may take up to two (2) hours to get through but there are computers there which allow you to browse the government website for jobs and relevant details that you could possibly need. You will get a letter size printout of the social insurance number which you must guard with your life. Someone could quite literally steal your entire identity with just that number.

You must be in the country for three (3) months to get your health card but a key requirement at the time of application for the health card is proof of address. As part of the process, you will need two documents proving you live in the province. I recommend that you have your drivers license and another being official mail received by you at your address. The easiest route to getting official mail is a bank statement which is why the second thing I'd suggest you do is to open a bank account. A bank account and a credit card will not only help with proving address for the purpose of your health card but will also parachute you on your journey to building good credit. Good credit is everything in Canada and as newcomers we must start from scratch and then maintain a good credit rating. Do some research beforehand to identify the bank with the best rates and packages for newcomers and then take your COPR and Social Insurance Number with you when going in to open your account.

Drivers License + Car/ Car Insurance

The topic of the drivers license actually falls within my recommendation for the first five (5) days but this is a whole beast on its own. My first job in Canada allowed me the opportunity to be licensed for home and auto insurance. I seldom use my knowledge of insurance to advise persons in a personal setting but this book provides me with a platform to educate persons on this very important topic. For that reason, I am guiding you as it concerns two things: getting your license quickly and how to ensure you do not commit, even inadvertently, insurance fraud as well as to understand how to get your insurance rates as a newcomer to be as steady as possible.

As a new immigrant to Ontario for instance, you have sixty (60) days from your date of landing to continue driving on your overseas license. Most provinces have a graduated licensing system. For Ontario, the classes follow the path of a G1 (learner) License followed by the G2 (intermediate) then a full G license. For Alberta, the learner license is a Class 7 license then the intermediate license is the Class 5 GDL (which is actually short for Graduated Driver's License) and then the full Class 5 license. Visit the ministry of transport website for whichever province you are in and become knowledgeable about road rules and signs. In addition, if you are in Ontario, download the G1 Test Genius Ontario app on your smart device and continually test yourself to ensure you know both (road rules and signs). Most provinces also have handbooks that you can read to help prepare yourself as well. As soon as you feel ready, visit the nearest Drive Test Centre with your driving abstract in hand and you will pay for and complete your test. In the unfortunate event you fail on your first attempt, you can do it multiple times on the same day until you pass. You will however have to pay for each attempt, of course.

Specifically for Ontario, if you submit the drivers abstract from your home country (if your home country has that agreement with Canada) and pass the learner driver portion of the driving exams, you have the option of going straight for the G (novice class) license or to the G2 (intermediate class). If you fail the G on your first attempt you have to do the G2 before being able to go for the G another time. I will leave the decision regarding which to do first, entirely to you. The G2 is assessed easier and it is said that some examiners are overly critical of newcomers going for their G and mark harder than usual. My original instructor in Barrie had told me this before we had our first class and encouraged me to change to the G2 to avoid the likelihood I would get someone who felt that he/she would have to mark me twice as hard as a newcomer coming from a country where we drive right hand drive vehicles on the left side of the road. He explained that it was just smarter to do the G2 first. Of course, I felt like taking a chance because after all, I had so many years of experience driving and I believe that I am very observant and defensive driver. I also knew persons who got examiners who were very professional and objective on their first attempt and got their G straightaway. Unfortunately, my experience was not like theirs, I believe that my examiner purposefully failed me for a fault that was not my own. When it is your time, choose whichever you feel more comfortable doing and just go for it.

If you do choose to do the G2 first, just know there is no waiting period after doing the G2 and you can go for the G when you feel ready. Some may think the G offers ultra-low insurance rates but that is not necessarily the case. With my G2, I currently pay $3000 CAD less than a friend of mine who got her G straightaway. Years licensed is the rating factor that is related to actual licenses and so regardless, you would have difficulties getting a dirt cheap rate anyway! This is not to say that a full G license is not appealing to insurers or that your rate may not be a bit better than the G2 driver in certain cases. What separates the G license though is the fact that the holder of a G license can drive on all major highways whereas a G driver licensed for four (4) or more years should be in the vehicle while a G2 driver is operating the vehicle on major highways. That doesn't always seem to happen here though.

Getting an exam date within a reasonable period of time is the hardest thing you'll have to do in the first couple of weeks especially if you land near a holiday like summer. I did my G1 on May 8, 2019 and the earliest exam date for the road test was June 18, 2019. A friend I met at work taught me a trick however which I applied as my exam date strategy and found myself with so many options. At one point, I had the option of choosing a time for the following morning which I opted not to take and when I eventually did my exam and passed it, I had actually selected that date the Friday evening for my exam Monday morning. The key is to first book an available date and pay for it. Chances are, your date will be far off but, as long as location is not an issue for you, you can constantly go on the drive test website, select 'reschedule' and scroll through the drive test centers within reach to see if any dates become available. Oftentimes, persons cancel or reschedule and their spots become available but these dates go fast. Do not be dismayed if when you select a date and time the system prompts you that the time has already been selected by someone else. Keep clicking. On August 2, 2019 I got September 20, 2019 and I kept rescheduling by clicking earlier dates at different locations even passing up dates I felt were too close and wouldn't allow me enough time to practice. Then, on that blessed Friday I found an open slot at a great location for the following Monday in mid-August.

After you get your license it is time to purchase your car. Please please please get an all wheel drive vehicle. Honda Civics are perhaps internationally the most popular starter vehicles but different vehicles are rated based on their risk so that may not be your best bet. I selected a vehicle based on how well it does annually on safety (less collision, accident benefits and liability claims) and the infrequency of certain perils such as theft for instance. In Jamaica, the Honda Fit and Toyota Axis are two vehicles which attract thieves. Comprehensive coverage (fire, theft, vandalism etc) for vehicles like these will be more expensive than comprehensive on some other vehicles hence higher rates.

On the topic of insurance, note that while car prices are probably hands down better than they are wherever you are migrating from, insurance is not. Insurance itself is about risk and from a business standpoint, insurance is a risk sharing pool where persons pay premiums towards the losses that the insurance company might inevitably have to pay out for the year. In simple terms, as a foreigner, you are seen as a bigger risk and your rate will reflect the relevant risks involved. Very few insurance companies consider years licensed outside of Canada and the USA. What are some of the rating factors to consider aside from years licensed? Age is a factor and understandably so. Were you a very experienced and careful driver at 18 or 22 years of age? Doubtful. Usage will also be a factor used to determine your rate. Please do not simply put a ridiculously low amount to save on cost and please do not lie and say the vehicle will be used for pleasure when you intend to drive it to work or school. Yes, it will be a cheaper rate but should you get into an accident and it is determined that you were on your way to or from work or school, your claim might likely be denied. Remember too that there are single vehicle accidents especially during winter so do not go the dishonest route only to lose out.

In this same vein, territory determines insurance rates as well. Even before I migrated, I had heard of persons using addresses of friends and family in rural areas to secure cheap insurance rates. Yes, some rural areas will be cheaper than urban areas but as I said before, in a claims situation your claim can be denied, and you would be found to have committed insurance fraud. This is very unattractive to insurers and you might then find yourself no longer qualifying for the company's regular book of business and then offered to instead take part in the alternate insurance market for high risk clients. The rates in that market are ridiculous! Reports are pulled by insurance companies when you start out with them and generally on an annual basis upon renewal. A part of the report displays your postal code. It is therefore easy for an insurance company to know if you lie about your address based on patterns. Some companies may not make a big deal of it but others may not desire your business. Further, using rural area codes sometimes comes with more expensive rates in a number of cases. My initial postal code and current postal code would have persons think it wise for me to use the old one since it is Barrie (semi-rural Ontario). The thing is, Barrie gets way more snow than in the GTA and has lots of slope-like roads. The likelihood of accidents, even single vehicle collisions, is therefore higher in that area than in the GTA. While doing your research on places to live and which vehicle to buy, do some research on Vehicle Rating Groups (VRG) to determine the ideal vehicle for your needs and circumstance.

Another way you can find yourself in the alternate market is through tickets. No matter how minor the tickets are, having three (3) and in some cases two (2) tickets or at-fault losses/ accidents may put you in a position where you no longer meet the company's regular book of business. Even with one (1) ticket, your insurance premium will be much higher because clients are surcharged for having that kind of risk and it will remain the case for three (3) whole years until the ticket eventually falls off your record. At-fault losses remain on your record and affect your premium for six (6) years. For that reason, my driving speed has been drastically reduced since migrating because I do not need a ticket to come up on my report each year when my insurance is being renewed by the company.

When anyone thinks of Canada, some of the words that readily come to mind are: cold, ice, snow, and wind chill to name a few. Most Canadians will tell you to 'put on winter tires as soon as the first snow falls', please listen to this advice. Some persons opt to drive with their regular all-season tires throughout the year but, two (2) days before I managed to get my winter tires on, I literally skidded all the way into oncoming traffic after trying unsuccessfully to get my car to stop at a red light. Fortunately, the other motorists and I survived without accident. Just preparing for winter alone could cost you a lot just to ensure you are commuting safely to and from work as a motorist so this is something you have to start factoring in and preparing for.

In preparation for my first Canadian winter, I got snow tires put on my vehicle and paid $106 CAD for the actual work to take my all-season tires off and put my winter tires on. Note: My four (4) all-season tires and four (4) winter tires are all on their own rims. My cousin said I was so fortunate because I actually got these Michelin winter tires as part of the deal from the car dealership. To purchase winter tires and get them on rims costs way more. In fact, just for a set of Michelin winter tires, you're looking at about $450 CAD and these tires usually have a lifespan of 2-3 years. A set of four (4) very basic rims will cost at minimum $270 CAD. I have observed that a number of Canadians seem to keep their tires on separate rims as opposed to removing tires from rims seasonally to avoid the added expense of removing them each time they need to be rotated. If the tires are not on rims, you can expect to pay over $170 each time (winter and spring) to have them put on rims and on your vehicle. I also installed a remote starter for my car to help me get my car warm before I leave my office in the evenings. The starter cost me a little over $600 CAD. For having snow tires though, I did get a discount on my insurance policy which seems to be pretty standard across insurance companies. However small this discount is, get your snow tires and ask about this possible discount.

Settling In

Living Conditions

As I would have shared earlier on, I literally had a handful of relatives in Canada and so I just could not muster up the courage to ask them to allow me to stay with them until I was able to get on my feet. I sent out what felt like a hundred resumes especially in Edmonton and Calgary where I was set on moving to and had even provided IRCC with Edmonton as my city of arrival as a permanent resident. I listed my local number on my resume and application letters until

I was told that employers seldom call unless you are in the country and then I started listing contact numbers for my friends. After realizing that time was running out and I had not gotten any interviews or job offers, I started looking for jobs in the Greater Toronto Area of Ontario. A family friend had indicated to my mom upon her visit to Jamaica that I could stay with her in Barrie (Ontario) until I got on my feet. I was terrified of this idea because quite often these arrangements go sour and I really did not want to be in the awkward position of being seen as a burden to anyone.

Having no other choice, I reluctantly took the offer and ended up staying with her and her children for almost two (2) months. I contributed financially to the household in the best way I could and spent my days looking for work. For those two (2) months, I avoided turning on lights and never turned her television on because I did not want to cause any increases to her electricity bill. To this day, I am immoderately grateful for the roof over my head for those two (2) months and eagerly welcomed the opportunity to go on my own as any grown person would.

I was encouraged by a number of persons to get a small place, preferably a basement apartment and for a while, I was reaching out to almost all the landlords for available basement apartments that looked presentable. For most, the fact I was a new immigrant was a huge turn off and I came to learn that some new immigrants are even expected to pay up to a year in rent as security. One real estate agent encouraged me to pay at least four (4) months rent upfront which was troubling to say the least. Rent for basement apartments ranged from $1200 to $1800 and of course the lower the price, the more inferior the quality of the apartment. I contacted a few landlords for viewings and strangely only one welcomed me to do the viewing. The living area was stunning but the bedroom could hardly fit a twin size bed and I found a long strand of brunette hair in the freezer. Having left my own home back in Jamaica, I decided that comfort was important for me and so moving into a basement was just not ideal for me. I love my peace and quiet and even more so, I believe my home should be my safe place so I moved away from basements and straight to looking into actual apartments and condominiums (condos).

I managed to find a beautiful apartment unit and got busy purchasing my furniture. There were many days I was extremely down in spirit but coming home to my own safe space always calmed me. As it turned out, my apartment costs just about two hundred ($200) more than it would have cost me in a basement which can get extremely cold and where the noise from upstairs can get unbearable. What if you just cant afford an apartment though or, what if you actually have children and need multiple rooms which will cost even more if in an apartment or condo? In that case, I'd advise you to get a basement apartment. Places go fast so make sure you are ready to jump at viewings and try to have proof of funds and the required down payment handy.

Employment

Even if you have a doctoral degree, do not assume you will automatically be able to secure a job in your field or at the level you were at prior to migrating. I have encountered a number of Canadians who, due to the fact they are not as well travelled as many who live outside of Canada, believed that the native language of Jamaicans is not English. Colleagues and clients alike were often confused by my accent when they first heard me speak because 'Jamaican' just did not click when they heard my voice. This now normal reality for me pushed me to develop a better understanding of why some potential employers think twice before shortlisting foreigners. The truth is that many believe that foreigners will have a hard time communicating with or being understood by their clients, that the work culture is a stark difference across countries, and that 'we' immigrants will take a bit more effort to polish and perfect for the role. This may sound unfair but I have interacted with other immigrants with whom conversations were extremely difficult because of the language barriers that exist.

Humility is your secret weapon and being willing to start small will potentially position you for success. Approach your job search with a new lens and new tools. Simply sending your resume with all your accolades and degrees and fancy experience will not cut it. We are at a distinct disadvantage and so you will need to start getting your face out there. If you are a shy person, un-shy yourself! Research job fairs in your city and/or neighboring cities and approach hiring officers with questions and discussions. Treat the five (5) minutes or whatever time you get as an interview and leave them wanting more; they should have a desire to learn more about you and should want to invite you to an interview. When I went to my first job fair, I had tons of relevant questions for the hiring officers and I made sure they saw that I was not only an asset but someone who wanted to be certain that their company was a good fit for me. One of the hiring officers ended up commending me and told me that I stood out from everyone who visited their booth that day simply because while others just wanted to know the salary and start date and those kinds of things, I wanted to know the company on a more intimate level.

Another great starting point to look into is joining a job finding club. The Canadian government provides a number of these clubs with funding to offset their costs. The club I participated in had all day presentations on topics of interest such as labour laws in Canada, work culture, interview and resume preparation to name a few. Many of these clubs also arrange networking mixers to allow participants the opportunity to meet and greet influential persons in the community. In addition to this kind of support, some job finding clubs help you to tweak your LinkedIn profile and to design cards for your personal branding. In British Columbia, I have heard of organizations which help immigrants to get placed in jobs that are related to their field of study.

For myself, I am still in the process of figuring out if I want to stay in my field or branch out into other areas I had explored years ago, like academia, or perhaps something completely new. A part of the reason for my state of uncertainty is the difference I noticed with how things are done in Canada. I have seen a lot of research jobs that my resume would be a perfect match for BUT these jobs often require a level of competence in a part of research methodology that I have been so out of touch with because that is not a requirement where I am coming from. In fact, that area is a job in and of itself in Jamaica. Similarly, persons holding specific degrees (example: Social Work) are unable to work in their field until they are licensed to do so by the province. Something I have been looking into and would definitely encourage persons in these kinds of situations to do is to research and apply for a bridging program in your area of specialization. There are bursary opportunities for short term study in Canada and you will find that having Canadian education on your resume will boost your job search tremendously.

Volunteering is also a huge thing in Canada. Many employers issue at least two (2) days in your leave allotment for volunteer work in your community. Now imagine how volunteer work will look to a potential employer. Don't get me wrong, I am not advocating for you to pretend to be interested in volunteerism and do so only for the gain. Rather, I am promoting the identification of something that you enjoy doing that will have a positive impact on the lives of others in some way. That must mean something to you. Let's say you are an IT Specialist, volunteer with a group that helps children or even adults to learn Microsoft Excel and the array of tools available at our disposal through this simple feature on most (if not all) computers these days.

Finally, take the time to tweak your job applications. I must admit that I am not great at this, because when you are desperately hunting for a job, you have so many applications to send out and time always appears to be running out on you. Ensure every application you submit to a potential employer is targeted, specific and view it as your one and only opportunity to get in. Most employers use the Applicant Tracking System (ATS) to shortlist clients. No longer are HR officers sifting individually through resumes but this is all computerized. For that reason, all key words need to be present from the job posting and your application needs to demonstrate who you are and why you are a great potential employee. While you wait, continue searching for other opportunities and keep your fingers crossed but be wary of job scams. Don't get too excited when you get a mail to your Indeed inbox about a 'work from home' opportunity paying you over five thousand dollars a month or an email offering a job you did not apply for but which asks that you submit your social insurance number. I get at least three (3) spam calls each month even from persons claiming to be calling me from 'Service Canada' or 'Canada Revenue Agency' regarding my social insurance number that I need to provide them with so they can discuss steps with me that I need to take to prevent legal action. Welcome to Canada!

In Conclusion: Testimonials

The following are testimonials shared by a handful of persons in my 'newcomer community'. Hopefully, the stories will be helpful and encouraging so that you are mentally prepared for this journey ahead of you.

Andy

I was an experienced Marketer, Marketing Officer to be exact, with a first Degree, ready to make that next jump but the family wanted a new challenge. Me being "Mr. Jamaica", a title my friends bestowed upon me because I was always against moving out of Jamaica, I waited and waited and waited until I slipped and said "why not?" one night and the wife ran with it.

The process for Express Entry was relatively easy although it did require research and skimming through forums but the information was out there and so there is zero need to pay consultants or expensive lawyers (I believe). Once you follow the processes and instructions, things can be seamless.

My wife is stronger than I am, I must say. She's more open and probably now missing Jamaica much less than I am. We moved here on September 2, 2018 with my wife being 4 months pregnant. At the time, we had never been to Canada before. We were just two lovers embarking on a crazy adventure. Luckily we had family, family like this is a godsend, people who genuinely want to help you transition, she had an extra room so we took that, no complaints about living conditions. Transportation was also good (give thanks for google maps 'eh!). The job situation, now there's the challenge, a friend of mine put me on to an employment agency that makes the transition for newcomers easier, sadly the benefit I received from this is confirming that I know how to do interviews or write my resumé, and at one point they wanted me to dumb it down. The good thing though is that they do offer mentors for newcomers with some corporate experience, this I do find valuable. You get to speak with someone in your field who can communicate a thing or two and this can only add value to your network right? In Canada, Network! Network! Network! And after that you better do some more networking. 'Tis the same thing we (Jamaicans) call having links.

Employment challenges, weather challenges, failing my driving exam the first time (with my 13 years of driving experience 🤦‍♂️) missing home, it's good to have a cry if you ever get overwhelmed. Hiring Managers may not explicitly say it but the lack of "canadian experience" will be an excuse, there's no way to get around that but you guessed it, networking. Kudos to anyone who comes along and finds something immediately in their preferred field, the usual route is to find a filler job so you don't exhaust your slush funds.

The weather can be depressing when it soaks in, you don't see the sun for weeks at times and that's where the real depression kicks in for me, this dark grey weather ain't it when you're knee deep in winter.

I was confident I would pass the driving exam up to the day, that is. On the day, a wave of "what if?" came over me and I downright got an empty brain when I got around the steering wheel. It was all me and my tears en route home, in the back seat of my instructor's car. Wife was still pregnant at the time so I needed to get the Drivers License so I could buy a car and move her around easily. I felt like I was failing big time!

Missing home was (and remains) my biggest issue. I'm the 'go to Portland (home) and chill for the weekend' person, the 'go to Hellshire on a whim simply for the fish and festival once or sometimes even twice a week' kinda person. And all this? Gone! I'm also the 'link up with friends and family a lot' person, so not having all that was a real bummer and a huge adjustment to make. Thankfully I have my wife and son who bring me much joy each day.

My advice to a newcomer; *NETWORK* and network some more. Seek out the information that you need, it's there. It really is. Never be afraid to ask questions and approach people who you think might add value. Practice your "elevator pitch" and if you're not the 9-5 kinda person, SEEK OUT HOW TO START A BUSINESS! It's not like home where there's a ton of import fees etc at the wharf, so it's a bit easier to get material or whatever from abroad. It could also be a service. Thing is, Canadians will pay for their services, once it's getting done on time and being done well. Capitalize on whatever talents you've been sitting on. Find out if you have any old friends nearby (lol), it will help to keep you sane when you link up most times, connect with family, you'll be glad you avoided the work-home-work-home routine.

For me, I'm still facing some challenges, personally of course. It hasn't been smooth sailing, at all, I've started a business but it hasn't launched yet because I wanna do it RIGHT and some suppliers haven't been convincing. But I will say this; coming to Canada to make more money, of course it can be done, 100%. You can make it, but coming to

Canada is not a silver bullet to "happiness", that's just me though.

Kevin

I came to Canada in 2018 for school. Of course that was not the initial plan because my wife and I had done the necessary steps to go the Express Entry route but that simply did not work out for us. The process seemed difficult at first but after checking it out further I discovered it really wasn't. I applied for school and after getting accepted, I applied for a study permit. My wife and children moved with me.

We arrived early with the aim of finding a place to live and we were in for a very very rude awakening. Due to our non-existent credit history, landlords either wanted up to six (6) months worth of rent as 'security' or overlooked us altogether. In fact, after finding a place we liked, we had to pay $12,000 CAD down. Imagine $12,000 CAD just for somewhere to live for a few months.

Before migrating, I recommend that persons start looking for realtors online to get an idea of available places for rent. Use Kijiji with a grain of salt, to see how you can find reasonable spaces. Kijiji normally has some good options but definitely some scams as well, so keep an eye out and be careful with your funds. If you do not have family or friends to stay with, book an Airbnb while you figure things out for the first couple of weeks. Transit is efficient, so in between the local buses, GO buses, Uber and other ride sharing services, commute wont be much of a problem especially if you live close enough to the bus routes.

I have since found employment after finishing school so my family and I ended up moving from Toronto to Fort McMurray in Alberta. This is definitely a different scenery from what we became accustomed to but my job pays really well and cost of living is really reasonable here. In addition to this, the place is beautiful and it is a great place to raise our children. I am not sure what the future holds but I am enjoying every bit of my Canadian journey so far…. Both the bitter and the sweet!

Mereike

My spouse had been recruited in Jamaica by a Canadian company that had come to Jamaica to hire power line technicians. He relocated in 2013 and I opted to wait until he got things settled and we were sure of such a big move. The company dealt with everything for us, his work permit initially and then our permanent residence. Eventually, I joined him and I landed in Canada on August 8, 2014. There were no direct flights to where I was going (the rural parts of Alberta in High Prairie) so I travelled from Jamaica to Toronto, then from Toronto to Edmonton, had to overnight in Edmonton then flew from Edmonton to Grand Prairie where my spouse came for me and we drove for two hours to High Prairie. I was beyond exhausted.

I was not homesick because I was happy to get to see my spouse, tour the area and get familiar with the place I would be calling home. I was content with this move but given that my spouse had to move about to different parts of Alberta for work and I was home alone at times for up to two weeks and there was little to do in High Prairie, I started to get lonely. Just recently, he and I were laughing about how things were at that time. Those were the days we watched every single movie at the theatre because that was basically the only fun thing available to do in High Prairie. Aside from that, there were fairs or an occasional circus that would come during holidays. I was so bored that I found myself back to what I had been used to doing in Jamaica, volunteering. I volunteered at a local hospital while awaiting our PR to be processed and finalized. We spent two years in High Prairie and during that time, we ushered in the birth of our son, Kyle, in December 2015. The local hospital there did not have a maternity ward and so we journeyed to Peace River where my son was delivered after a very scary delivery. I am still so grateful that, after all the complications, the care was exceptional and that he survived. We were overjoyed because of the blessing that our son was and still is.

In the midst of us celebrating the birth of our son, the company made a decision to downsize and a number of men were laid off including my spouse. He then had to seek work elsewhere and I was desperately in need of spending time with my family since I had just given birth so I returned to Jamaica for six months. He found a job in Manitoba and that was where we spent the next two and a half years before moving to Toronto in 2019.

For any newcomer to Canada I'd advise that person to have adequate savings because you may not get a job right away and you will need money to keep you afloat until you can pick yourself up. Do your research! Canada is big and there are many systems in place which may confuse or overwhelm you. Sometimes it may feel like jumping hoops and can get frustrating. It will also be very important to have a good support system because if it wasn't for my spouse, I'd have moved back to Jamaica a long time ago. When considering where to live, if you have children, research schools in the area. I now live just a few minutes walk from my son's school and a number of other key amenities so that makes my life so much easier. We are also now in a house instead of an apartment like we had been before, and so I get to have my washer and dryer inside my house. I was so tired of struggling with my laundry to the basement of my apartment to do my laundry every week.

Canada is a beautiful place. I don't know if I will live here for the rest of my life but while I'm here I am making use of the opportunities and allowing my son to enjoy all that is available to him. Be prepared to be alone and depressed sometimes, be prepared to miss your family especially when it gets cold during the winter months. Be prepared to find complex processes sometimes that will overwhelm you because, the truth is, Canada gives the beauty and the toughness all in one. Good luck on your journey.

Shines

Everybody hears of the glitter and the glamour of Canada but my story is far from that. My Canadian story started in 2008 when I was 20 years old and working in the tourism sector in Jamaica. I had my own apartment and everything young men would consider important at that age. I wasn't remotely thinking about leaving Jamaica and as a matter of fact, I didn't know where Canada was or even how a visa looked!

My journey to Canada started with my mother who became really worried after a heated turf war had started in my community. Many young men in my age group had become involved in gangs and even though I was not one of them, my mother started losing sleep because every time she heard of a youngster being murdered, she would be afraid that it was me. At the time, I was working varying shifts and so I'd get home sometimes at 2:00 AM or as late as 4:00 AM. Personally, I wasn't afraid because these were youths I would have probably gone to school with and so I knew them and they knew me. I didn't think I had anything to worry about but my mother was another story.

One day my mom saw an advertisement in the local newspaper about studying in Canada and she called me about it. I had no interest to be honest. After a taste of independence, it is hard to start feeling the urge for school again but during my weekly visit to her for our usual Sunday family dinner, she asked again if I would be interested. She reminded me that my grandma was in Canada and that grandma had a townhouse so I'd even have somewhere to stay. I promised her I would look into it just to get her to change the topic.

While I forgot about it, she got to work. She started researching the process, filling out applications, requesting exam results and school leaving certificates from me and I realized she was really taking this school thing serious. I had a number of passes but also had a few grade fours (4) in my school leaving exams which was a 'fail' so I really didn't have high expectations. Months later, I got the shock of my life. The school replied and indicated that my application was accepted. At the time, I was required to pay $500 CAD for them to hold the space for me. We paid the fee and things started to sink in. I was going to study in Canada. By then I started wondering wah me really a get myself inna (translation: what I was really getting myself into). My parents and I pooled funds and I paid $6000 CAD of the $11,000 CAD annual tuition fee for a degree in hospitality and tourism management so I was good to go! On July 1, 2008 (Canada Day), I left Jamaica for my new home in Scarborough, Ontario (Canada). That was my first time on a plane, first time outside of Jamaica, first time everything!

Grandma worked mostly nights so for that summer I was always home alone and bored because I had no friends in the area. I used all the money I had to buy phone cards to call home just to have company sometimes. By September however I started school and found myself integrating well because I played football for the school and got opportunities to travel for games across Canada. My parents and I managed to find the remaining $5000 CAD

through loans for my second semester but by my
econd year of the programme, we were all out of
money. I rushed to foreign without a Plan B. Plan
was to finish school and get permanent residence
but with plan A out the door and with year one (1)
of a three (3) year visa down, I needed to figure
things out quickly.

At the time, I was in a relationship with a Canadian born to Jamaican parents but she didn't know my situation and I didn't want to disclose that to her. I couldn't afford to seem like I was using her which I wasn't. I actually had a female friend who wanted to marry me to help me get permanent resident status in the country but I wasn't sure I could do that. Dem ting deh can get dangerous iyah! (Translation: those things can get dangerous). I eventually confessed to my girlfriend and she ended up telling her parents who surprisingly took it quite well. They tried to help us figure out avenues and then we decided to just get married. I was 23 years old. What did I know about marriage?? Anyway, we got married and the paperwork started.

As a married man, I now had to find a job to support my household. That was another problem because I had no 'papers' yet and so I could not legally work in the country. I started looking for cash jobs all over the province just to make ends meet. I worked in construction fixing basements with a trade man at one point which was rough. I also did work fixing fences and also doing lawn aeration which was more than just the actual rough work. We had to walk from house to house to try and convince people to allow us to do it for a fee. Some people closed doors on us which was really embarrassing but the money had to be made so I had to brave up and take it like a man. I remember one man paid me $20 CAD for the whole day when I was to have made $80 after working for that day. It was unfair but when people see you are doing cash jobs they pick up that you're not legal so they try to take advantage of the situation. What you going to do? Report him? Fight him?

At one point I got a cheese factory job at a site owned by some middle eastern people. The owners of the factory provided a bus that met us at a designated place and it took me one (1) hour to get to the pickup spot from my house. The bus ride was three (3) hours to the location and three (3) hours back and we had to do this daily. This job was similar to what many know as farm work. We lined up daily and they assigned us to different parts of the factory. The factory was extremely cold because we were dealing with dairy and so the temperature had to be kept very low. For whatever reason, I wasn't very lucky because I always seemed to get the end of the line. I remember the first day I was on the line rapidly packing all the boxes. After what felt like six (6) hours, I realized we were only one (1) hour in. My hands started to fail me and I knew this type of work was not for me. Big man ting, mi did waah cry (translation: On a serious note, I wanted to cry). I saw an older lady crying as she was probably realizing what I was too… we took ourselves out of our relatively comfortable jobs back home and came to this. It didn't take long before I quit that job. I juggled cash jobs for the next few years trying to make ends meet.

Within these years of struggling, imagine being sick and wanting to go to the doctor. That was another crosses! (Translation: problem). Healthcare in Canada is free BUT remember I didn't have any legal status so of course, no health card. I couldn't afford medical bills so friends and others recommended clinics that accept people without any paperwork. These doctors seemed young and like they were amateurs fresh out of school. They were probably stuck between volunteering and experimenting and I was a very ready science experiment. You think a joke? (translation: You think I'm joking?) They asked nothing about status but the fact you had no health card it was a given. They attended to us and we took what care we could get. As Jamaicans say "Beggars cant be choosers".

Fast forward to getting my PR card in 2012, four (4) years after moving to Canada as a student. I went back to Jamaica for a month because of how homesick I was but I had a new lease on life. I returned to Canada and started doing an apprenticeship programme in scaffolding which took a year. By 2013, a friend told me about a scaffolding job in the province of Saskatchewan. I experienced the coldest temperature ever while there.... -60 C! It was so cold that persons were banned from leaving their homes until the temperature improved. I have also worked as part of a team across other provinces including Ontario, British Columbia and Alberta at different times over the years. Of course, this type of work is outdoors so my work is not luxurious… no sit down in soft chair type of thing. We work for hours outside in rain, snow, sleet… just about every type of weather condition.

I realized quickly that skilled tradesmen make good money in Canada. Although it is very rough work, the money definitely keeps me going. Today I am still in the business of scaffolding. I work in Alberta but live in Ontario so you can say I am bicoastal. I can now take care of myself and my family with ease and invest. Because of my rough path here, I try to guide persons who I meet who come to Canada without any documentation. Sometimes I have to laugh when I look back at the experiences I had here but fortunately I knew I had to make something of myself and I didn't stop until better came.

My advice to persons who want to come to Canada for school is to make sure you have your money. Things and times have changed. If by chance you come to Canada and find yourself without status for whatever reason, like dropping out of school due to insufficient funds or even a failed work permit, make sure you have a plan B. Don't get sidetracked especially if you come to Toronto. Friends and partying often suck people into a dangerously fake lifestyle. You'll find yourself caught up in the liquor and the designer shoes and not a decent roof over your head. Deal with your papers first!

Another bit of advice: don't run to get a drivers license and get caught up in that either. If you run red lights or get other kinds of tickets, it is easy to get deported. The bus system is efficient especially in the urban areas so just be humble and keep your head on your body (translation: keep focused). Work and save and then work and save some more. It may start slow but it is a guarantee.... things will turn around for the better. This is the best country to move to. Healthcare is free and many opportunities are here once you're willing to start small. In the words of Sizzla Kalonji, "simplicity we use to survive".

Nathalee

I arrived in Canada the evening of April 20th, 2019 at the Toronto Pearson International Airport. I was expecting to be picked up by a family friend who offered to allow me the opportunity of staying with her and her children in Barrie, Ontario until I got settled into life in Canada. I had done a lot of research prior to 'landing' and had organized everything I felt I would need at immigration, including my confirmation of permanent residence, my bank reports (since I literally only took three thousand Canadian dollars ($3,000 CAD) with me, and a piece of paper I used to neatly write the address I would be staying at which I gave to the officer with whom I spoke to make the process as simple and brief as possible. After all, you are only a permanent resident after you are granted entry, so 'nervous' was an understatement. I journeyed to Barrie with my family friend and I was in the house of God for Easter Service the following morning.

There were a number of things I knew I had to do as soon as possible and one of those things was my social insurance number. I visited Service Canada, waited for almost two (2) hours (since there were many other persons waiting to be seen), and left with my social insurance number in hand. I walked to a bank that was recommended by a few friends as ideal for newcomers. Unfortunately, I was told, explicitly, that my confirmation of permanent residence was illegible and that both that document and my social insurance document seemed fake. I felt so embarrassed that I asked for the matter to be escalated and even when that was done, I left the bank feeling like I was being turned back because I was a newcomer from Jamaica.

My next stop (about a week later) was to the Drive Test Centre where I sat the G1 exam. In retrospect, I wish I had done that as soon as I landed but everything about my journey has been a true test and has sharpened my resilience in so many ways. I had gotten a letter from the Ministry of Transportation in Jamaica prior to moving; it indicated the status of my Jamaican driver's license. I passed the G1, opted to go straight for the G and was surprised to learn that the waiting period to do the road tests were ridiculous. I waited for six (6) weeks before I was able to do the road test.

After six (6) weeks in the country, I visited Service Ontario and got the process started for my health card. During this time I also enlisted in a job finding club where I socialized with other newcomers and participated in sessions to help me understand Canadian work culture and the laws in place to protect employees in the workplace. That experience also taught me about commute in Canada as I got a rude awakening with the bus system. After attending a newcomers job fair in downtown Toronto on May 25, 2019 I got offered my first real job interview in Canada and subsequently my first job. I was so thrilled.

Things started taking a turn for the worst immediately after I started working. At the time, I had moved from Barrie and was temporarily staying with one of my mom's friends because the family members I had been building relationships with lived much further away from where I got the job. Even so, I was traveling for over two (2) hours one way each day. My mother's friend was extremely kind and I got home to encouragement and delicious meals daily. I barely slept for the first two (2) weeks as I prepared for a licensing exam I had to sit. On my second day on the job, I failed my class G driving exam. I was almost at the end of the exam when I was penalized because of a decision I made to preserve life when a motor cyclist appeared between the two (2) unbroken yellow lines to my left as I was approaching the filter lane to turn left. My decision cost me my G license, much to the delight of my examiner who failed me for 'obstructing traffic'. At that time I didn't know I could contest it given the situation but I took my loss and moved on.

While preparing for my extremely difficult licensing exam, I started apartment hunting. I noted ads posted outside apartment buildings regarding vacant units and scoured kijiji and other sites to identify available basements. Given my pay scale, it was important to ensure that I was in a living space that fit my budget. I was having immense challenges with being considered because I had no experience renting in Canada and of course because of my accent which seemed to turn off most landlords of a 'particular' race. By then, reality was kicking in, that I would probably have to resort to a most undesirable space. I searched high and low (literally) until I eventually found a lovely and spacious apartment, and decided I was taking it despite the price. I knew it was better for me to step out in faith and take what I want with the hope, nay, the expectation, that my earnings would eventually match that expense.

Two (2) weeks into my new job, my dad passed away. I was a mess! Fortunately, he died hours after my exam and I was able to complete and pass the exam before learning of his death. In the midst of grief and confusion, I moved into my ‘dream apartment’ and one of my closest and longest standing friends, Pedro, flew to Toronto from New York to help me move in. In the rental vehicle I had for the weekend, we drove to every Homesense store to get all the subtle décor and posh cushions to make my home as comfortable and homely as possible. By the time he left a few days later, I was back to mourning and feeling completely lost. The day before my father died, I had finally gotten through to IRCC and was told that there was an error with the address that was entered for me in their system; even though I had literally written the address and gave it to the officer when I landed. I had to call back the day after my dad died to query my options for leaving the country seeing that an emergency travel document was not the most ideal option for me. I was told that I can actually enter the country without my PR card but via land and I was sent an actual document regarding how that is done. This is not the same as flagpoling.

Basically, had I not received my PR card in time and needed to travel, I would have had to return to Canada via private passenger vehicle. In my case, the best bet for me would have been to travel from Jamaica to Buffalo (New York) where my cousin would come from Canada and pick me up to transport me back across the border to Canada. Fortunately, I did not have to go through that trouble. My PR card was re-routed and arrived prior to my travel date so I was able to purchase a regular one-way ticket back to Toronto, having already purchased my ticket to Jamaica. Despite the fact that I was only employed for two (2) weeks prior to my dad dying and not being sure if I should simply return to Jamaica, I was awed when I found out I was actually being given bereavement days from my company. There was so much I was dealing with at the time that I felt like a fish out of water and I was so messed up that I even panicked and failed my second driving exam the morning after I returned to Canada from my father's funeral. How eventful my life always is!

At that point I started to sink deeper and deeper into depression. I found myself harboring self-destructive thoughts and I cried more often than anything else. I became reclusive and pessimistic and I felt foolish for uprooting my life and tossing myself into a space where I had to fight to maintain my sanity. My commute was rough and I often found myself running behind buses if they were departing earlier than scheduled and in other cases being completely confused about which way was east or west, and north or south. I started having what appeared to be arthritis and I was constantly exhausted. I barely had time 'to scratch my head' as elderly Jamaicans often say. The high point of my days was the view from my top floor apartment and I spent all of my free time by myself at home. By mid August I realized I was not improving and that I had lost hope. I recall walking to meet my first of three (3) buses after work one evening and started to remind myself of God's word and His promises for my life. I began talking to Him loudly as if He was walking with me up the incline and I saw a few persons in their vehicles looking bewildered. In the midst of my conversation with God I got a word to write a book based on my experience that will help persons who wanted to migrate to Canada. I had always been passionate about 'writing' as a child but I never thought I would end up sharing anything about myself that would make me feel vulnerable, or that I could write a book that would impact anyone. Nevertheless, I started writing down everything I wanted to include in this book and found myself so caught up with this calling that I started challenging myself to document my experiences through videos and photographs.

I re-did my driving exam (for what was my third attempt) mere days after that life changing encounter with God and passed. That evening I went vehicle hunting and hopped from dealership to dealership until I found my vehicle. The rest is history.

Evaluation after Month Six

Fast forward to my birthday in October 2019, six (6) months after starting my journey as a permanent resident in Canada, I have no regrets. I am nowhere near where I want to be but I am so proud of myself and so thankful to God for taking me through it all. My biggest takeaways after month six are:

1. Your savings is everything! I had no idea how important the funds required by IRCC was until I realized that within four months I had spent almost $20,000 CAD just to get settled and make myself comfortable. Everything in Canada costs money and

having savings is a cushion for any newcomer. Persons that I know who opted to live with family members or friends often complained of how uncomfortable things became. My mother always taught me as a child to never overstay my welcome. In Canada, never overstay your welcome. Nothing beats having your own space and thriving on your own.

2. Job finding clubs, job fairs and networks are probably the most useful tools in any job seekers toolbox. There was so much that I learned at the club that I was a part of and my first job came about because of my attendance at a job fair. I was able to refer other newcomers at my company and help them prepare themselves in order to secure jobs there as well. I believe that as newcomers, regardless of ethnicity or race, we have to look out for each other because we know how difficult it often is when we first land.

3. Build a circle of support. Having genuine friends and family is sometimes all that can

take you through the transitory period of starting over and settling in. Canada has a lot of holidays that promote family, including Family Day, Thanksgiving and other days. Given how tough it will be as is, your support system will provide a welcome distraction. For me, my family often came for me to take me to stay around them where I would feel less alone and develop a sense of community. I also found a church family that has been so warm. There are different religious or ethnic groups which meet and help support their peers so however you identify, get involved 😊

4. Ensure you have even one peaceful aspect of this adventure. For me, that was my apartment and its gorgeous view. If you don't mind the cold or tiny rooms and probably a weird landlord, get a basement apartment but if you are like me, look into getting a decent apartment. For some persons, their comfort is getting a nice car. I had a Honda HRV in Jamaica before I migrated and I purchased a Mazda CX3 GTX (luxury trim) when I finally got my

> vehicle in Canada. I took the luxury trim because I wanted All Wheel Drive, the moonroof, and heated seats. One of my friends purchased a vehicle for almost $15,000 less to avoid the expense but then she didn't have those features. Some would wonder why I'd take an apartment that cost most of my salary for the month and a luxury model vehicle but as I said before, everyone believes in something or someone and for me, I believe in the miracle working power of God to elevate me and reward me for the exercise of my faith.

I appreciate your belief in the value of the experience I had to share and the advice I can provide you with in starting over. Migrating is not easy and will definitely come with many ups and downs. I hope this guide and the collective experiences I've sprinkled throughout this guide was useful and that you will keep in touch through my various social media pages. I have also been rounding up a supportive group of immigrants who, like myself, are ready and willing to share with you. I am here to help.

Cheers! 🥂

About The Author

Nathalee is an experienced researcher and policy professional turned 'newbie' author. She is passionate about issues of social importance and, based on her personal experience as a newcomer to Canada, the study of migration has become a new research interest for this Sociologist. Eager to help others, Nathalee has formed a community of newcomers committed to sharing their experiences and advice with persons who have decided to pack up and move to Canada.

Notes

Made in United States
North Haven, CT
31 October 2021

10718026R00074